CREATIVE LIVES

Charles Dickens

NEIL CHAMPION

Heinemann
LIBRARY

www.heinemann.co.uk/library
Visit our website to find out more information about **Heinemann Library** books.

To order:
☎ Phone 44 (0) 1865 888066
▤ Send a fax to 44 (0) 1865 314091
▥ Visit the Heinemann Bookshop at www.heinemann.co.uk/library to browse our
catalogue and order online.

First published in Great Britain by Heinemann Library, Halley Court, Jordan Hill, Oxford
OX2 8EJ, a division of Reed Educational and Professional Publishing Ltd. Heinemann is a
registered trademark of Reed Educational & Professional Publishing Ltd.

OXFORD MELBOURNE AUCKLAND JOHANNESBURG BLANTYRE
GABORONE IBADAN PORTSMOUTH NH (USA) CHICAGO

Designed by Tinstar Design (www.tinstar.co.uk)
Originated by Ambassador Litho Ltd.
Printed and bound in Hong Kong/China

ISBN 0 431 13982 2
05 04 03 02 01
10 9 8 7 6 5 4 3 2 1

British Library Cataloguing in Publication Data
Champion, Neil
        Charles Dickens. – (Creative lives)
        1.Dickens, Charles, 1812-1870 – Juvenile literature
        2.Novelists – English – 19th century – Biography – Juvenile literature
        I.Title
        823.8

Acknowledgements
The Publishers would like to thank the following for permission to reproduce photographs:
Dickens House Museum: pp5, 8, 10, 16, 19, 27, 30, 32, 33, 34, 38, 39, 43, 47, 50, 51, 52;
Illustrated London News Picture Gallery: p28; Mary Evans: pp7, 12, 17, 21, 24, 31, 37, 40, 41,
45, 53; Museum of London: pp14, 48; National Portrait Gallery: p4; Portsmouth Museums
and Records Service: p9; Ronald Grant Archive: p54.

Cover photograph reproduced with permission of Hulton Getty.

Our thanks to Andrew Xavier of The Dickens House Museum for his comments in the
preparation of this book.

Any words appearing in the text in bold, **like this**, are explained in the Glossary.

Contents

'The novelist of his age'

Charles Dickens is remembered today as one of the greatest and most popular writers of the novel ever to have lived. He has appealed to readers of all kinds, all over the world, since the publication of his first novel in 1836. Nearly all the important people of his day read at least one of his novels – politicians, fellow writers, philosophers and economists, social **reformers** and so on, as well as the mass of ordinary people who adored Dickens's writing. Even Queen Victoria was a fan.

The spirit of the age

Dickens captured the spirit of his age in both a profound and entertaining way. He wrote with wit and humour, but he also wrote about the everyday tragedies of life he saw around him. He put these all into the context of **Victorian** society.

During Dickens's lifetime, Britain moved from being a rural and agricultural country to being the world's first industrial giant. This rapid change put enormous strain on all levels of society. Rural farmworkers moved to cities and became the **urban** poor. Traditional landowners with inherited money were eclipsed by the new factory-owning millionaires. Politicians were struggling to keep up with the demands made by the emerging **middle classes**, who were becoming

This painting of Charles Dickens was completed in 1839 by Daniel Maclise. Dickens was by then a married man with children and several published books to his name.

increasingly wealthy, mostly at the expense of the poor. There were few laws to help workers, and they were cruelly exploited in the name of profit and progress. Because Dickens became the biggest-selling novelist of his day, he became a powerful voice that people had to listen to. He had the great skill of creating memorable characters and **dialogue** while also addressing themes of social concern. In his private life he helped various charities, including schools for the children of the poor. As we shall see, he had his own personal reasons for doing this.

Real life and fiction

Dickens used many of the thousands of experiences and encounters from his real life in his works of fiction, altering the names of people and places, and sometimes exaggerating situations to make them more funny or tragic. That is why the *Daily News* commented the day after his death in June 1870, that he was 'The novelist of his age.' The journalist who wrote these words was not only referring to the fact that Dickens was the greatest of the English 19th-century novelists, but also that he was the writer who most captured the spirit of the times in which he lived. His own life and the age in which he lived were tightly intertwined, more so than with most writers.

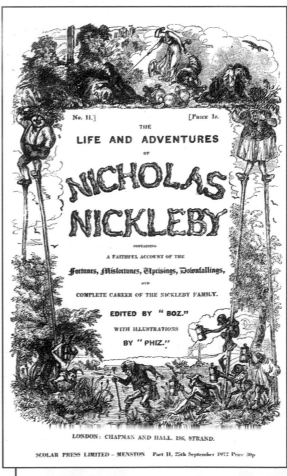

The frontispiece of Dickens's second full novel, *Nicholas Nickleby*, published in monthly numbers in his magazine, *Bentley's Miscellany*, between 1838 and 1839.

5

He constantly worked his own life into his novels, which is why a greater understanding of his life can make reading his novels much more rewarding. In all he wrote fifteen full novels, some of great length, as well as many journalistic and travel pieces, and short stories. He invented over 2000 characters in his books, many of whom have become famous in their own right – Oliver Twist, Mr Bumble, Ebeneezer Scrooge, Little Nell, Miss Haversham, Mr Micawber, Betsey Trotwood, to name just a few.

Dickens's life and times

Most of Charles Dickens's adult life was lived through what we call today the Victorian period. Queen Victoria came to the throne in 1837 and reigned until 1901. This period was one of unparalleled growth in terms of the population of Britain and the economy. The **Industrial Revolution**, which had started towards the end of the previous century, had really taken off by the time Victoria became queen. Britain had become the 'workshop of the world' and its empire was to become the most extensive the world had known.

Sources of information

In his middle age, Charles Dickens told his friend John Forster many things about his childhood. Forster went on to write the first biography of the great novelist, publishing it four years after Dickens's death, in 1874. He called it, simply, *The Life of Charles Dickens*. From this source we have many firsthand accounts of what Dickens thought about things and what he remembered about his early life. We also have the memories that other people had about Dickens – his relations, his nanny, teachers from the schools he attended. Many of these accounts were written after Dickens had become famous and wealthy from his writing, and therefore have to be treated with some caution. We also have letters written by and about the great man. Together, these firsthand accounts provide us with very valuable material on Dickens's life and character.

An image of industrial England at its worst. Factory owners frequently used children as their workforce, exposing them to dangerous machinery, long hours of work and paying them little.

THE
WHITE SLAVES
OF
ENGLAND.

Dickens responded to all the change that was taking place across Victorian society by writing about it. He showed how different characters from different economic backgrounds could react and use, or fail to use, the new opportunities that unrestricted **capitalism** was presenting. He contrasted the new greed and ambition that were fostered in this climate with older values of love, loyalty and self-sacrifice. Often he used the contrasts to show how funny or absurd people can be – he is one of the greatest comic writers in the English language. At other times he highlighted the tragic consequences of the collision of different worlds and values – how so often the poor, the defenceless and the weak are crushed by the strong and greedy, by progress in a very general sense. Throughout his life, Dickens championed the underprivileged. He saw so much abuse and mistreatment of people in the name of profit and progress going on around him. He wrote skilfully to entertain his readers, but he also wrote to try and change society for the better.

The mask of childhood

Charles Dickens was born on 7 February 1812. His father was John
Dickens, a clerk in the naval pay office in Portsmouth; his mother was
Elizabeth Barrow. Both were from the lower **middle classes**. Although
not poor, John Dickens's income was only enough for the family to live
modestly. However, he was irresponsible and extravagant with the
money he earned, and cast the family into debt and financial crisis time
and again, until he eventually ended up in Marshalsea Debtors' Prison.
These were all events that left deep scars on the developing personality
of young Charles. He was humiliated by the downturn in his family's
fortunes, and the theme of humiliation crops up often in his novels.

Charles Dickens's mother, Elizabeth Barrow, is shown on
the left. In 1810, her father stole money from his
employer and fled abroad. John Dickens, on the right,
the novelist's father, also had continuous money problems.

Charles Dickens was the second child in what was to be a large family. His sister, Fanny, was just over a year older than Charles. Six other children were born to the Dickenses, two dying very young – little Alfred, aged only a few months, who suffered what was described as 'water on the brain' and Harriet, aged three, who contracted **smallpox**. Their deaths were to remain in the memory of the novelist: childhood deaths occur frequently in his writing and are treated with a mixture of sentimentality and uncomprehending fear.

Dickens was an unusually sensitive and visually aware child, and he stored away the memories of these different times – the people he met, the places he lived and visited, sights and smells of various towns and cities, the language spoken by those around him and so on.

Charles Dickens's first home – 13 Mile End Terrace, Landport, Portsmouth. He was born here on 7 February 1812.

9

A view of Rochester in north Kent, showing some of the marshes and the River Medway that the young Dickens came to know so well. He set the opening of *Great Expectations* in this area.

Early memories and influences

Dickens's first memories hark back to his homes in the Chatham and Rochester region on the north Kent coast. His father had moved his family to this area in 1817, after a short spell working in London. His employer, the Royal Navy, had appointed him to offices at the dockyard in Chatham. It was in this landscape of seaside towns and marshes, both open to the elements of wind and rain, that Dickens set several of his novels. This includes his first (*The Pickwick Papers*) and his last (*The Mystery of Edwin Drood*, where he changes the name of Chatham to Cloisterham), showing the continued and deep importance of the area in his imagination.

The theatre

It was in and around Rochester that the young Dickens came across such powerful **catalysts** to his developing imagination as the theatre. He was to say of himself, 'I was… an actor and a speaker from a baby.' There are several accounts of people in later life hearing the writer at work behind closed doors acting out the characters in his novels as he composed their **dialogue**. The whole world of theatre, plays, pantomime and the **music hall** was to remain a source of joy and entertainment to him all his life. He was taken to the Theatre Royal in Rochester by his family and later to theatres in London itself – the home of the theatrical world – only 50 or 60 kilometres (30 or 40 miles) away. He called the Theatre Royal 'the sweet, dingy, shabby little country theatre', and its smells of lamp oil and sawdust left their mark on his memory. It was here that he saw his first Shakespeare performances, as well as popular 19th-century **farces** and **melodramas**. Young as he was, Dickens absorbed the atmosphere of powerful make-believe and illusion that art brings to our lives. He even experimented with writing his own plays, from the age of nine.

The world of books

The other big influence outside family life was that of literature. Dickens took to reading, as he took to the theatre and acting, from a very early age. He first went to school in Chatham at a Dame school in Rome Lane. He left it in 1821, moving to a larger school in Clover Lane run by a young **Baptist minister** called William Giles. Giles seems to have recognized in the young boy something special. He taught him

> " William Giles, the schoolmaster at Chatham, remembered the young Charles Dickens as being *of a very amiable, agreeable disposition… Charles was quite at home at all sorts of parties… and birthday celebrations.*' He was quite often called upon to sing little songs *'in a clear treble voice'* at such parties. We get a view of a sociable Dickens, rather than the lonely, melancholy boy that he so often dwelt upon in later life. "

An engraving of a 19th-century Dame school, such as the one that Dickens attended in Chatham up until 1821. As the name implies, these establishments were often run by older women, who had few teaching skills.

English grammar, essay writing, handwriting and reading verse and prose aloud. He also lent him books to read. David Copperfield, one of Dickens's most important characters from the novel of the same name, says, 'Reading... was my only and my constant comfort.' This echoes the author's own feelings. His father also had many books which he devoured with a great appetite.

Dickens once wrote of the room in a house in Chatham that: 'From that blessed little room, where *Roderick Random*, *Peregrine Pickle*, *Humphrey Clinker*, *Tom Jones*, *The Vicar of Wakefield*, *Don Quixote*, *Gil Blas*, and *Robinson Crusoe* came out, a glorious host, to keep me company. They kept alive my fancy... – they and *The Arabian Nights*, the *Tales of the Genii*.'

These were the names of the popular novels of his day, and were also names of the heroes in them. They coloured his young and impressionable imagination.

Daily life

Life for the Dickens family would have been a mixture of chaos and routine. Mrs Dickens would have had a difficult time looking after so many children, especially as the spaces between her pregnancies were not long. John Dickens would have had the refuge of his work at the naval pay office.

Running the household would have taken a great deal of Mrs Dickens's time. Things that are relatively simply household tasks today, such as cooking, shopping and cleaning, would have taken a lot longer, even with the help of domestic servants. During this period, there was no running water or sewage systems to carry waste away. The average age that people lived to was around 40 years – disease and sickness were an ever-present worry, and childhood was a particularly vulnerable stage of life.

Trials and tribulations

John Dickens was promoted at the naval pay office in Chatham in 1821 and a year later was sent back to London, to work at Somerset House. All the family except Charles moved to a house in Bayham Street, Camden Town, which is now part of London, but in the early 19th century was still surrounded by fields with only a view to the distant spires of the city. It was just about walking distance for John Dickens to his office from home. Charles remained in Chatham, living at the house of his schoolmaster, William Giles, for a further three months, no doubt finishing off his education there. However, the time came for him to catch the 9.30am coach and horses out of Chatham, bound for London. There is a marvellous description in Dickens's novel *Great Expectations* of the main character, a young man called Pip, seeing London for the first time as he arrives from the north Kent coast by coach. It no doubt recalls Dickens's own feelings of awe and wonder, mixed with some fear, as he arrived in the big city.

The Elephant and Castle area of London in the 1820s. Coaches and wagons, including the mail coach carrying letters and parcels across the country, can be seen.

The loss of schooling

The ten-year-old Dickens did not take to Camden Town. The house in Bayham Street was modern, built of yellow brick and terraced. It was cramped, 'a mean small tenement, with a wretched little back-garden on a squalid court,' Dickens reported to John Forster many years later. He came to see his life on the north Kent coast as one of innocence and ease, where he was looked after and well educated. In London, life changed radically. Suddenly there was no school to go to. It came as a great shock to the book-loving boy, who was showing so much promise under the guiding hand of William Giles. Dickens recalled, 'As I thought... of all I had lost in losing Chatham, what would I have given, if I had had anything to give, to have been sent back to any other school, to have been taught something anywhere!' The loss of his education at this time and the neglect into which he had fallen stayed with him as a painful memory all his life. He says of his father at this time, 'he appeared to have utterly lost at this time the idea of educating me at all... So I degenerated into cleaning his boots of a morning, and my own; and making myself useful in the work of the little house...'

Taking refuge

Looking back on this depressing period of his life, Dickens saw that he took comfort in books. He retreated into a world of fiction. This was his way of coping with the loss of his education, and with it the loss of his self-esteem. 'I should have been perfectly miserable, I have no doubt, but for the old books,' says one of his characters, David Copperfield, who finds himself in similar circumstances to his creator.

Exploring London

Dickens did not confine himself solely to his books. He started to wander the streets and lanes of Camden, looking out towards the great dome of St Paul's Cathedral a few miles away in the city, and over the roofs and spires of London. The extensive walking that he did through the city was a habit that stayed with him all his life. It gave him a detailed knowledge which he used to great effect in those novels that he set in London.

Bayham Street in Camden Town, London, where the Dickens family moved to live in 1822. Charles disliked living there, preferring the Kentish countryside.

So great was Dickens's knowledge of the great capital city to become, that we have today the idea of 'Dickens's London'. His novels use the city and its life almost as a major character in the plot. London itself became a subject for his writing. Elsewhere, writers were exploring in similar ways – for example, Bolzac (1799–1850) in Paris and Gogol (1809–1852) in St. Petersburg. The city was to become the single most important environment for their characters to inhabit. This reflects the enormous growth of certain cities in Europe and Russia at this time. But none grew faster than London, seat of power for the industrial giant Britain was becoming.

Visiting relatives

We have a mental picture of Charles Dickens at this time, as a young boy of ten or eleven years, now living in London, trying to adapt to his new circumstances. His family was growing around him and his father was as reckless with money as ever. Dickens took to visiting people, as a welcome diversion from his home life. For example, he visited his uncle, Thomas Barrow, who was renting a room from a bookseller's widow. His uncle had broken his leg, which was later amputated and a wooden replacement one fitted. The young boy was fascinated with this, and wooden legs became a peculiar feature in several of his novels. The widow was another source of books for Dickens and soon he was borrowing volume after volume to read into the night.

He also visited his godfather, Christopher Huffam, who was a sail-maker and ran a **chandler's** business from a shop in Limehouse in East London. Memories of such curious shops, selling all manner of things for the thriving shipping business on the River Thames, crop up in his novels. He was clearly fascinated by them. And, as with so many activities from the busy world of commerce and human interaction that he saw going on around him, he wrote of them with great accuracy and detail and from a great depth of feeling as a grown man.

London's busy docks in the mid-1800s. Dickens spent much of this time exploring the city, soaking up the sights, sounds and smells which he later used to great effect in his novels.

Debt and disaster

The year 1824 was not a good one for Charles Dickens or his family. In April of the previous year, his sister Fanny had been enrolled at the Royal Academy of Music in London. The cost of her piano tuition and lodging was 38 **guineas** a year, which was a large sum for her father to pay out of his annual salary of £350. But this was typical of his unthinking and misplaced generosity. Charles, who at this time was getting no education at all, was hurt by this lavish treatment of his elder sister. As usual, however, he kept his thoughts and feelings to himself. They appear much later in life in his writing, where he often sees young ladies as very privileged creatures, who are sometimes rather cruel and empty-headed.

Sliding into debt

By 1823 it was clear that the family needed somehow to increase its income. Dickens's mother took it into her head to open a school for young ladies. She rented a large house in Gower Street North and moved all the family there, putting up a brass plaque with the words 'Mrs Dickens's Establishment' on it. The venture was a disaster. Instead of adding to their income, it drained it – the rent was higher than in their last home, and no pupils ever enrolled at the school. The family took to using pawnbrokers' shops to survive. These were shops that lent money to customers who deposited (pawned) valuable personal belongings until the money could be paid back. Charles was often sent to pawn books and other items of value. He felt humiliated by these events. Pawnbrokers' shops, like so many features of his life, are written about in his novels with contempt. In later life he set about buying all the books he had had to pawn as a boy. Perhaps this was a way of attempting to regain his lost, disgraced childhood.

Warren's Blacking Factory

To further highlight the difference in treatment that the young boy felt he was being given compared with his sister, a job was found for him. He started work at Warren's Blacking Factory at Hungerford Stairs shortly before his twelfth birthday, in February 1824. He hated it. It was almost a five-kilometre walk one way from their home. He was put to work alongside **working-class** boys, one of whom was called Fagin, the name that Dickens was later to give to the rogue character who haunts Oliver Twist and runs a crime racket, sending boys out to pick pockets and worse. He called these boys 'common' and 'degrading'. 'No words can express the secret agony of my soul as I sank into this companionship,'

Warren's Blacking Factory at Hungerford Stairs on the River Thames in London. It was here that the twelve-year-old Charles Dickens was sent to work, a time he looked back upon with deep resentment.

he was to write later in life. The young boy who had taken to books and education, and who in Chatham had seen himself as becoming a 'learned and distinguished man' was now getting no tutoring and was working all day for six shillings a week. No doubt the family needed the money, but the contrast between his life and that of Fanny's was enormous. The work itself was unstimulating and repetitive – putting labels on to the jars which contained the black polish (blacking) for boots. Dickens would sit at his bench alongside the other boys, pasting the labels on all day long. It is typical of him that in later life he mentions that he eventually took some small pride in the fact that he became one of the best and nimblest workers there.

> " This terrible time in his youth was remembered by Dickens, who wrote *'even now, famous and caressed and happy, I often forget in my dreams that I have a dear wife and children; even that I am a man; and wander desolately back to that time of my life.'* "

Debtors' prison

Throughout 1822 and 1823, Dickens's father fell further and further into debt. He failed to pay the local rates (tax money) for paving and lighting, for example. He was arrested shortly after Charles had started work at the blacking factory, on 20 February 1824, for non-payment of a debt to a local baker, which amounted to around £40, a huge sum for the day. He was taken to a place called Marshalsea Debtors' Prison, off Borough High Street in London, where he would be kept until he paid off what he owed. This catastrophe seems to have hit the young Charles harder than it did his other brothers and sister. Fanny, who somehow managed to remain at the Royal Academy of Music, was cushioned from the blow. His other siblings were too young, perhaps, to be deeply affected. Charles felt once again the humiliation of his family and his own circumstances. He probably also felt some of the financial burden, even at the young age of twelve years. He was, after all, earning his living. Another character, Pip in *Great Expectations*, says, 'It is a most miserable thing to feel ashamed of home.' And this is what the young Dickens was feeling – isolated, humiliated and somewhat lost in the world.

Destitution

The family sold all they could, but eventually they had to give up the house and move into the prison to live alongside John Dickens until such time as they could pay the debts they owed. Charles was sent to lodge with a family friend, Mrs Roylance, in Little College Street, which he later described as 'a desolate place'. Once again he was on his own and reliant on himself. His isolation during this period must have been immense. He later moved to lodgings closer to the prison, so that he could have breakfast with his family before going to work at the blacking factory. His salary of six shillings a week barely covered the cost of his rent and food. He was often to go hungry, missing meals because he could not afford to buy them. His own and the family's fortunes had sunk just about as low as they could go. Their position was a short step away from that of the criminal classes, the underworld of London life that Dickens was to write about so convincingly in novels such as *Oliver Twist*.

Certain areas of London were notorious for crime. Here, an obviously well-dressed man is being assaulted and robbed in the street.

Back in the wide world

John Dickens's brother, William, paid off the debt to the baker. But John still owed money to other people. He finally declared himself **bankrupt** and had to go through the humiliating process of having everything he owned valued. He was finally released in May 1824, having spent over three months in prison. His mother died in the same year, and left John £450 in her will. But the family was in dire straits. They went to live at first with Mrs Roylance, but by the end of the year had their own house in Johnson Street, near Camden Town. John Dickens continued to work at Somerset House but these remained difficult times. He was also unwell, suffering from 'an infection of the **urinary organs**', a complaint that was eventually to lead to his death.

Fact meets fiction

As with so much that happened in his life, Dickens was later to write about prison and its effects on people and family life. His father, on one visit to Marshalsea, told him that a man whose income was £20 and whose expenditure was £19 and 6d, was a happy man. But if he spent £20 and 6d he was wretched. Dickens later put these words into Mr Micawber's mouth when David Copperfield visits him in debtors' prison.

Dickens in the wider world

In March 1825, John Dickens retired from the navy pay office on a pension of £145 a year. One benefit of this was that he took his son away from the blacking factory and put him back in school. The Wellington House Academy was in Hampstead Road, a short walk from their home in Johnson Street. In the next two years Charles blossomed. He recovered his high spirits and mischievous nature. He learned, amongst other things, Latin and the violin. He kept up his story-writing, circulating funny **sketches** amongst his school mates. One friend remembers, 'he was very fond of theatricals. I have some recollection of his getting up a play at Dan Tobin's house, in the back kitchen… we made a plot, and each had his part…'

Writing for a newspaper

John Dickens started a new career, writing for *The British Press* newspaper on parliamentary and **marine insurance** matters. Charles may also have started to contribute what was known as 'penny-a-line' copy (literally earning a penny for each line of print) on such things as local accidents and fires. Charles took to journalism like a duck to water. In fact he kept links with newspapers and **periodicals** all his life, which later came to include owning them. *The British Press* ceased to exist from October 1826 and by the end of the year the Dickens family were **evicted** from their house, being once again in debt. They managed to get it back later in 1827, by which time the fifteen-year-old Charles had left school 'to begin the world' as he wrote in a letter.

Dickens and betrayal

The theme of betrayal by women is a strong one in many of Dickens's novels. This feeling may have come from the special treatment given to his elder sister Fanny. He clearly felt that his mother betrayed him. She wanted him to stay on at the blacking factory rather than go to school. He wrote of this, 'I never shall forget, I never can forget, that my mother was warm for my being sent back [to the factory].'

London life

Charles Dickens kept up the habit of wandering the streets of the great city of London. He absorbed the life of the people he saw around him, taking note of their work – the oyster sellers, the piemen, little match girls, street conjurors, jugglers and acrobats, and robbers, called 'footpads'– and the lives of the rich, the tradesmen and the beggars, of whom there were many. He witnessed dog fights and cock fights, public hangings and brawls in the taverns. There were no railways yet in the city (these came in the 1830s and 1840s), but there were plenty of horse-drawn carriages. There was no public **sanitation**, and street lighting was very basic. We get a sense from his works of a rich and energetic place, full of violence and chaos, with moments of warmth and human sympathy.

A lawyer's clerk

In May 1827, at the age of fifteen, Dickens started work at Ellis and Blackmore, a lawyer's firm in Holborn Court in the City of London. His mother had arranged this through acquaintance with Edward Blackmore, one of the partners in the business. His salary was 10s/6d (ten shillings and sixpence) a week, but the work was routine, mainly administration – copying out documents and the like – and running errands through the streets of London. His employers soon came to realize just how well he knew these streets: 'His knowledge of London was wonderful, for he could describe the position of every shop in any of the West End streets.'

Dickens was to write often about lawyers, judges and barristers in his novels. He was rarely complimentary. Perhaps his most famous expression about it was put into the mouth of Mr Bumble in *Oliver Twist*: 'The law is an ass,' he exclaimed. *Bleak House* (written in 1852–53) deals with a long-running law case and its negative effects on the lives of many people, such as Richard Carstone, who dies as a result of his obsession with the case. Dickens contrasted the law's deadening effect (symbolized in the opening chapter of the novel by the heavy November fog that falls on London) with the warm love and self-sacrifice of characters Esther Summerson and John Jarndyce.

Here, a trial is taking place at the Old Bailey in London. Dickens knew about the law through his employment as a lawyer's clerk in 1827 and his father's imprisonment for bad debt.

Dickens and mimicry

An early skill that Dickens showed was that of being able to **mimic** other people for fun. It went hand in hand with his interest in acting and also with his ability to capture the character of a person in writing. He observed very closely people's **mannerisms**, and exaggerated them for effect. Fellow workers at Ellis and Blackmore benefited from the fun and games and remembered his skill: 'Dickens could imitate... the low population of the streets of London in all their varieties, whether mere loafers or sellers of fruit and vegetables, or anything else.'

Learning shorthand

Dickens knew that the law was not the career he wanted in life. He had enjoyed writing pieces for the newspaper and had always been good at writing character sketches and little plots for plays. So he set about learning **shorthand**, something his father had done for reporting on parliamentary sessions. What took most people years to learn, Dickens mastered in a matter of months. He was developing tremendous energy and application for hard work, something that stayed with him all his life. He was eager to do well in life and make his mark. He had also

Bleak House and the law

Dickens was always critical of the inhuman and self-serving processes of the law. He gives a gloomy picture of human life stifled by its slow workings in *Bleak House*. The opening pages paint a picture of fog-bound London, in which all lives are touched by this damp and disheartening atmosphere. It is a symbol of the state of the Courts of Chancery, where:

'On such an afternoon, some score members of the High Court of Chancery bar ought to be – as here they are – mistily engaged in one of the ten thousand stages of an endless cause, tripping one another up on slippery precedents, groping knee-deep in technicalities, running their goat-hair and horse-hair warded heads against walls of words, and making a pretence of equity with serious faces, as players might. On such an afternoon, the various solicitors in the cause, some two or three of whom have inherited it from their fathers, who made a fortune by it, ought to be – as are they not? – ranged in a line, in a long matted well (but you might look in vain for Truth at the bottom of it), between the registrar's red table and the silk gowns, with bills, cross-bills, answers, rejoinders, injunctions, affidavits, issues, references to masters, masters' reports, mountains of costly nonsense, piled before them...'

had too many brushes with poverty to want to slide back down the ladder towards nonentity. **Victorian** London could be a very cruel place for those with no money and no prospects. Crime was seen by some as one way out, but the penalties for being caught and prosecuted were harsh. Victorians believed that people simply choose to become criminal and that it was fair to treat those who were caught cruelly – many criminals were exported to Australia, and hanging was the penalty for more serious crimes. There was no social 'safety net' for those who fell by the wayside.

Charles remained with the law firm in the City for about a year and a half, having made himself useful to his employers and popular with the employees. But he was now all set to launch himself into a new career as a journalist.

The years of struggle

Dickens, for all his energy and dedication, was about to enter into one of the most difficult periods of his life. He was still living at home. His younger brothers Alfred Lamert and Frederick were at school in Hampstead. However, the family finances were still very bad. At the end of 1831, John Dickens was once again in court for not paying his debts. He had continued to work as a parliamentary reporter, but it was not enough. The young boys were taken out of school after a couple of years and Fanny was withdrawn from the Royal Academy of Music. She was lucky, though. She managed to get some employment at the Academy teaching music for seven shillings a week.

The constant moving from one home to another to avoid the **creditors** was still an unsettling feature of home life. Dickens was also still uncertain about his future. He left the law firm and became a freelance reporter. This satisfied him for a while, but it was hard work and largely unrewarding. He flirted with the idea of going into the theatre. He wrote to a playhouse in Covent Garden, saying that he had 'a natural power of reproducing in my own person what I observed in others'. He even got an interview, but was too ill to attend. He was eventually to turn his genius for observation and **mimicry** to the pen and not the stage.

Young love

In amongst all these worries came Dickens's first true and powerful encounter with love. The object of his affections was a young woman, slightly older than himself, called Maria Beadnell. She was the daughter of a banker and lived in a well-to-do area of London, in Lombard Street. He nicknamed her 'the pocket Venus', because of her small but pretty form. She looked down on the young suitor – as did her family, who were opposed to their relationship – but kept up a relationship with him from 1830 until 1833. It was a one-way affair, with Dickens besotted by her, and she enjoying the attention in a cold and distant sort of way. Dickens put some of his feelings into the fictional relationship between David Copperfield and Dora Spenlow, a similar young woman to Maria: 'She was more than human to me... I was swallowed up in an abyss of love...'

A portrait of Charles Dickens aged about eighteen. It was around this time in his life that he met and fell in love with Maria Beadnell.

Dickens would walk to Maria's house late at night after work and simply stand looking up, hoping for a glimpse of her. But here again was an example of betrayal by women. Looking back on this period, Dickens said that 'there never was such a faithful and devoted poor fellow as I'. He was made to feel socially inferior to her and unworthy of her. This no doubt fed his growing ambition to make something of his life and move away from his 'shabby genteel' background. (Dickens used this phrase to describe people who – like his father – had fallen on hard times, but liked to keep up appearances.) He was ready to take flight into writing fiction, in which he would put to use all the acute skills of observation, character analysis, humorous **anecdote** and scene-setting.

> " Some of the letters Dickens wrote to Maria Beadnell have survived. In one of them he gives us an insight into how she made him feel about himself and about how this fed his ambition to prove himself. He tells her about his *'own unimportance'* but that *'all that any one can do to raise himself by his own exertions and unceasing assiduity, I have done, and will do'*. We can hear his determination to succeed in these words to the woman who was dominating his emotional life. "

The solitary observer

In the spring of 1831, Dickens got a job reporting on speeches made in the Houses of Parliament for a weekly paper called the *Mirror of Parliament*. Its owner and **editor** was his uncle, John Henry Barrow. Dickens would go to the press gallery, where journalists could view the proceedings, and listen to the important Members of Parliament (MPs) of the day. This was a turbulent time in British politics, with the **middle classes** of the nation, now quite rich from the gains of the **Industrial Revolution**, pushing very hard for the **reform** of the parliamentary system. This system had benefited the **aristocracy** and other wealthy people with land for generations. But the big industrial towns, such as Birmingham, Manchester, Leeds and Liverpool, where hundreds of thousands of people now lived, were poorly represented by MPs. Things had to change, and the **Great Reform Act** of 1832 carried many of the **Liberal** plans through, extending the right to vote to many of the middle classes, while ignoring the demands of the workers. Dickens was in the thick of this, recording in **shorthand** for his newspaper the hurly burly of the House of Commons.

The press gallery in the House of Commons in London. Here Charles Dickens recorded the speeches he heard from the politicians of his day. He wrote them up in newspapers.

Starting writing

In 1834, Charles Dickens moved on and up in the world of journalistic reporting. He joined the influential **Whig** daily newspaper the *Morning Chronicle*, and received a salary of five **guineas** a week. He continued reporting on Parliament, but also started to travel across the country, recording election and campaigning speeches. He saw the industrial towns of the north for the first time.

In the same year he also started to work on his fiction in a serious way. He was separated from Maria Beadnell, and turned his considerable energies to writing. Over the next few years he was to turn all the solitary observing he had done of human life and character, from his earliest years and memories, into fine pieces of fictional composition, published eventually under the title of *Sketches by Boz*. Boz was a **pseudonym** that Dickens used when he gathered all these stories together, taken from a nickname for Augustus, his youngest brother. This collection, written through the first half of the 1830s, was published in various **periodicals** (the *Monthly Magazine* and the *Evening Chronicle*) and eventually in book form in 1836. It was, as Dickens's subtitle put it, 'Illustrative of Everyday Life and Everyday People.' Dickens had put together his genius for character-writing and scene-setting into an original format – that of short **sketches**. He combined the novelist's skills with those of the journalist, writing such pieces as 'The Beadle', 'The Old Lady', 'Our Next-Door Neighbour', 'Greenwich Fair', 'Private Theatres', 'A Christmas Dinner', 'Shabby-Genteel People', 'The Drunkard's Death'. He was learning his trade with these short excursions, preparing himself for the sterner stuff of writing much longer and complex novels.

> " The first piece of fiction that Charles Dickens had published was "
> called 'A Dinner at Poplar Walk'. It appeared in the *Monthly Magazine* in 1833. When he saw it in print, he *'walked down to Westminster Hall, and turned into it for half an hour, because my eyes were so dimmed with joy and pride that they could not bear the street'*.

First reviews

Sketches by Boz was given a very good reception by the reviewers of the day. One commented that it showed: 'a close and acute observer of character and manners, with a strong sense of the ridiculous and a graphic faculty of placing in the most whimsical and amusing lights the follies and absurdities of human nature'.

Dickens had captured the imaginations of the people of London with his very realistic (though exaggerated) portraits of life in the city. This collection of stories was to establish his reputation and displayed the unique combination of literary skills that have come to be called 'Dickensian' – the wonderful and colourful characters; the combination of humour and **pathos**, the grotesque and the sentimental; and the language itself, in part that of common speech, mainly from the mouths of the Londoners that Dickens heard around him.

First commission

Due to the popularity of this work, Dickens received some attention from publishers. One of these, Chapman and Hall, asked him to write what would become his first novel, *The Pickwick Papers*. He started to write in February 1836 to a tight deadline for the first instalment, which came out the following month. It was to usher in an age of monthly stories, all related and continuous in narrative, much in the manner of a **soap opera** on television today. The serialization of new pieces of writing was something that Dickens was to make a huge success of over the coming years,

The frontispiece of Dickens's novel, *The Pickwick Papers*. It was serialized between April 1836 and November 1837, and published in one volume in 1837. This set the pattern for most of his future novels.

A 19th-century printing press. Dickens benefited from improvements in the printing industry (which became mechanized and steam-driven). His books could be printed in bigger quantities and much faster than ever before.

building up an audience of readers always eager to find out what happened next in the lives of his heroes and heroines. Commercially, it was a very profitable way to publish his novels. In time it made Charles Dickens a very wealthy man indeed. It also affected the way in which he wrote those novels due for serialization – he needed to leave the reader in suspense at the end of each month's instalment, so that they would be keen to buy the next edition.

A huge success

The Pickwick Papers was a huge success. This was partly due to the rise in population in Britain and the increase in wages that many people enjoyed – there were more people with money in their pockets to buy periodicals and books than ever before. The national level of literacy (reading and writing skills) was also improving continually. People were keen to better themselves through reading and Dickens tapped into this feeling. He was also helped by technology. Printing presses and paper manufacturing had been transformed by the Industrial Revolution, which had brought in steam driven machinery for the first time. Also, transportation networks were opening up across Britain and the rest of the world, in the shape of steam trains and faster ships going across the Atlantic Ocean to the USA. All these things combined to make a mass audience possible for a writer like Dickens.

Marriage to Catherine Hogarth

Charles Dickens met his future wife through his journalistic contacts. Catherine Hogarth was the eldest daughter of the **editor** of the *Evening Chronicle*, George Hogarth. Dickens visited his house, and got to know Catherine. They became engaged in May 1835 – she was nineteen and he was 23. She was described by a friend as being 'a pretty little woman, plump and fresh-coloured, with the large and heavy-lidded blue eyes so much admired by men...'

They were married less than a year later, on 2 April 1836 at a church in Chelsea, in the Hogarths' **parish**. They took their honeymoon in Kent, renting a cottage in a village close to Rochester. Dickens was no doubt feeling far more secure in his life now. He was beginning to make money from his fiction, and was also being well paid for his journalism. These things in turn made it possible for him to marry. He and Catherine rented rooms in Furnival's Inn, one of the old **Inns of Court** in Holborn. At last he seemed free of his family (though in one way or another he was to look after his younger brothers all his life, especially Frederick, of whom he was very fond).

A painting of Catherine Hogarth, completed in 1846 when she was about 31 years old. She had married Charles Dickens ten years earlier, in 1836.

Family life

The Dickenses were to have ten children altogether. Charles tended to give his sons rather elaborate and literary names – Charles Culliford Boz, Alfred D'Orsay Tennyson, Francis Jeffrey, Henry Fielding, Sydney Smith Haldimond, Edward Bulwer Lytton and Walter Landor. His daughters had plainer names – Kate, Dora and Mary. The first child, Charles, was born on 6 January 1837. It was a difficult time for Catherine (known as Kate to her family and to Dickens). A letter from her sister, Mary, from this time makes the case: 'Poor Kate! It has been a dreadful trial for her... It is really dreadful to see her suffer... Every time she sees her Baby she has a fit of crying...'

She was probably suffering from depression, and living in the cramped three rooms at Furnival's Inn did not help matters. Dickens took Catherine and the family back to their honeymoon cottage in Kent, to help her recover. However, Catherine was to have a hard time with the births of each of their children. Most were to live into adulthood – good statistics for the middle of the 19th century, when **infant mortality** was still very high, though on the decline. No doubt this was helped by the increasing prosperity of the family through the 1840s, when most of their children were born. However, Dora died in infancy (of 'convulsions'), causing tremendous grief to both parents. Dickens stayed up all night watching over the body of the dead baby, and finally broke down in grief, something he very rarely did in a life marked by determination and control.

Daniel Maclise's painting of four of the Dickens children, painted in 1842. They are, from the left, Kate, Walter, Charles and Mary (known as Mamie).

Dickens and work

Charles Dickens had a morbid fear of financial insecurity. He knew at first hand how dreadful life could be without the safety of money and influence. His education, the one thing that as a boy he took great pride in, was totally disrupted. In the years that followed his marriage he worked like a man possessed, driven by the genius he had in him and haunted by the terror of poverty. He left the *Morning Chronicle* in November 1836 and started editing a new magazine, *Bentley's Miscellany*. He also launched himself in what spare time he had into writing more novels in instalments. *Oliver Twist* (today one of his best-known novels, helped by the fact that it has been made into a musical and a highly acclaimed film) was serialized in *Bentley's Miscellany* between 1837 and 1838. This was rapidly followed by *Nicholas Nickleby* (1838–39), *The Old Curiosity Shop* (1841) and *Barnaby Rudge* (1840–41). Sales of his books by this time had reached around 100,000 copies, fantastic figures even by today's standards. He was now the most popular and talked-about novelist in the land.

A photograph of 48 Doughty Street in central London, where Charles Dickens and his family moved in 1837.

Finding a family home

With the arrival of their first child, the couple made the decision to look for somewhere more spacious to live. Dickens was now a recognized literary figure and his income was growing. They had moved into 48 Doughty Street by

April 1837, for an annual rent of £80. It was a large town house on four floors. They took on a cook, housemaid, nurse and servant. The Dickenses had clearly arrived in the prosperous **Victorian middle class**. They were to remain at this address until December 1839 when, after the birth of their third child, they moved to a very large house at 1 Devonshire Terrace, Regents Park. Dickens was by then a wealthy man.

Tragedy

Catherine's sister, Mary, had become a very good and close friend of Charles. She had often stayed with them over the months of their marriage. When the Dickens family moved to Doughty Street, she moved in with them, having a room of her own in the household. However, she died suddenly on 7 May 1837 in their house, after returning late at night from the theatre. The story goes that she collapsed from heart failure and died in Charles' arms. She was seventeen years old. Dickens grieved inconsolably. He even missed his deadlines for the monthly instalments of both *The Pickwick Papers* and *Oliver Twist*. This was an extremely rare event in his life, as he was very strict with himself about work deadlines and commitments. Mary had obviously meant an enormous amount to him. He wrote on her gravestone, 'Young, beautiful, and good.' In his mind she represented an image of positive feminine attributes such as warmth, beauty and loyalty, as opposed to the negative ones, which he had experienced as betrayal and rejection.

---

48 Doughty Street

This address is today home to The Dickens House Museum (see page 63 for details). It can be visited in London or on the Internet. You can take a tour of all the floors, seeing Mary Hogarth's room, Dickens's bedroom, the drawing room, study (where Dickens wrote some of *The Pickwick Papers*, most of *Oliver Twist* and all of *Nicholas Nickleby*), dining room and library. It provides a great insight into the workings of a prosperous middle-class home in the first half of the 19th century.

Travels in the USA

On 4 January 1842, Dickens and his wife went by steamboat from Liverpool to North America. Dickens had been thinking for a while that a trip to the USA would be useful to him. The idea was to tour both Canada and America. He was a great admirer of the relatively new republic and had been encouraged by correspondence with the great American writer Washington Irving. Dickens was to say that, 'if I went, it would be such a triumph from one end of the States to the other, as was never known in any nation'. He was attracted by the thought of meeting in person the large American audience that his books had attracted over the years. No doubt the thought of increasing the sales of his books was a part of his plan as well! He had a few things to say about slavery, viewing the contrast between whites, who were protected by the Declaration of Independence, and the lives of black slaves as a 'monstrous lie'. He also criticized the annoying habit of US publishers breaking **copyright** and bringing out **pirate editions** of his works.

Preparations

He had prepared himself for the trip very well, having bought numerous maps and 27 guide books! He left the children in the hands of his younger brother, Frederick, and insured himself for the sum of £5000. In all, he and Catherine were gone six months, taking in parts of Canada, then going on to the great American cities of Boston (where he had breakfast with the poet Henry Wadsworth Longfellow and had first contact with his adoring public), New York (where he dined with the writer Washington Irving), Philadelphia, Washington, Baltimore and St Louis, to name but a few of the places he visited.

> " In a letter to John Forster, his friend and future biographer, Dickens wrote: '*How can I give you the faintest notion of my reception here; of the crowds that pour in and out the whole day; of the people that line the streets when I go out; of the cheering when I went to the theatre; of the copies of verses, letters of congratulations, welcomes of all kinds, balls, dinners, assemblies without end?*' "

At a speech he gave in Boston, the philosopher and poet Ralph Waldo Emerson was in the audience. Emerson left a picture of the energetic Dickens: 'too much talent for his genius; it is a fearful locomotive to which he is bound and can never be free from it nor set to rest… He daunts me!'

However, as the trip went on, Dickens and his wife began to tire. This is not surprising. In New York he took to his bed for three days. He had from youth grown accustomed to his own space and moments of solitude. On a tour like this he had no time to himself. He sat for his portrait, he spoke at dinners

A portrait of Henry Wadsworth Longfellow (1807–1882). He was a great American poet and professor of modern languages at Harvard University. Dickens met him on his first American tour in 1842.

in his honour, he had literary breakfasts, and in amongst all this he also found time to visit America's orphanages, asylums and prisons. He did this out of his own interest and also with the eyes of a journalist. He wanted to see how this young democratic country dealt with its poor and 'problematic' people.

Criticism

Although Dickens was generally well received wherever he went in the USA, he did not have it all his own way. American newspapers began to think that he was in the States purely to make profit out of the country. While this was not entirely true, there was enough for them to go on. He was stung by criticism that he read in the papers and wrote in a letter of 1842, 'I am disappointed. This is not the Republic I came to see.'

When Dickens visited New York in 1842, many people flocked to see the great novelist. His books had made him an extremely popular figure.

They had travelled out by steamboat but Dickens had not enjoyed the excitement of such a new mode of transport (the first steamboat crossing of the Atlantic had taken place only four years before). They returned from New York, leaving on 7 June, aboard the *George Washington*, a sailing vessel, landing at Liverpool docks some three weeks later.

American notes

Dickens wrote up his account of his travels in the USA in a book he was to call *American Notes*. It is based largely on the letters he wrote to his friend John Forster back in England during his time away. Forster was to write a biography of the great man in 1874, after his death.

Despite the endless round of social events given in his honour, there was no disguising the fact that the novelist was disillusioned with America. He was critical of the American newspapers, **sanitary** conditions in some cities, piracy of his and other writers' text and, especially, American manners!

Not surprisingly, the book did not go down well in the USA. People were so angry with what Dickens said about them as a nation that the book was publicly burned at a theatre in New York!

A cartoon of Charles Dickens and his friend and first biographer, John Forster. Dickens is on the right, and top right. Forster wrote his life of Charles Dickens between 1872 and 1874, after the novelist's death.

The novel years

When Dickens returned from the USA in the summer of 1842, he threw himself back into work with his characteristic energy. There were great drains upon his money – his growing family, his father (always looking for handouts from his son) and his two younger brothers (who seemed unable to find work for themselves); and also upon his time – mostly self-imposed, through his involvement with **copyright**, setting up **writers' guilds**, charitable functions, public dinners at which he was guest of honour, society balls and so on. He was also writing what would become *American Notes*, his experiences from the recent tour, and *Martin Chuzzlewit*, a novel that was to be partly set in the USA. The first instalment of the novel would be ready in December 1842. He established a pattern where he would work for the first week or two

A painting of Broadstairs in Kent, England. Charles Dickens started taking his family on holiday to this seaside resort from 1837 and continued to visit it up until 1851. Today there is a Dickens museum there.

of each month on the text, get this to his printer, then correct the **proofs** in the second half of the month ready for publication. In amongst all this he found time to start what would become an annual event with his family – taking them to Broadstairs in Kent for a holiday.

An American visitor

He had one major interruption in the autumn of 1842, when the American poet, Henry Wadsworth Longfellow, suddenly visited him. Longfellow had described Dickens as 'a glorious fellow... a gay, free-and-easy character with a bright face'. He would visit the novelist again in 1856 and 1868.

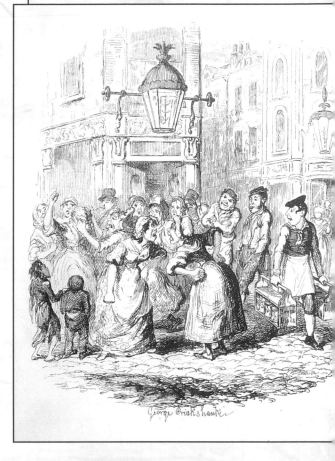

The slum area of Seven Dials in London, around the middle of the 19th century. Most people avoided these places, as they were populated by the poorest and most desperate inhabitants in the city.

Dickens entertained him with visits to Rochester and Bath, and some of the London sights. This included taking Longfellow to the notorious 'rookeries'. These were the slums of London that bred so much crime, especially amongst the young. Only one in three children went to school in London at this time, which meant that unscrupulous adults had plenty of children to use for their criminal activities. London had been growing rapidly – by 1847 it was to have a population of over two million, making it the largest city in the world. Longfellow was not spared the dirty, disease-ridden and depressing underbelly of the great city. It was, after all, where Dickens had some of his roots.

The volume of his work

Over the next three decades, Charles Dickens would write another nine large and complex novels and many shorter pieces of fiction, including ghost stories and stories for Christmas. He would keep up his journalism, his public functions for charities such as housing projects, orphanages and **ragged schools**, and he would travel again, to continental Europe and to the USA for the second time, for a very profitable but also highly exhausting reading tour. He did not often let up, driven as he was by ambition coupled with fear of poverty. He never felt that he was a rich man, and by the standards of the **aristocracy** or the new owners of industry, perhaps he was not. But he never had to go without, and was always able to support his large family and all the hangers-on. He had to keep writing.

Minor setbacks

American Notes did not go down well in the USA. Dickens was too critical of the society he found there – including some of the institutions he visited, such as the prison, which he thought too lenient on the inmates. *Martin Chuzzlewit* was also not as successful a novel as its predecessors had been. It was, to some extent, different. Dickens was maturing, and in this novel he portrays his main characters in a subtly different way to those of his early novels. There is more **psychological** depth and realism; characters are shown to be influenced by and to adapt to events happening around them. They show themselves capable of change through circumstances. However, this shift away from obvious characterization – in which character types can be easily defined as 'good', 'hard done by', 'evil', 'stupid and scheming' and so on – to something altogether more subtle, was not immediately appreciated by his audiences. He was to tell his friend John Forster that in spite of the low sales, 'I think *Chuzzlewit* in a hundred points immeasurably the best of my stories.'

It is a novel that Dickens planned and structured far more than his earlier works. In many ways, it marks a transition to a more 'crafted' approach to writing, showing that Dickens was changing as a writer.

Making good

With his story *A Christmas Carol*, however, Dickens showed once again that he had a way of knowing just what his audience wanted. It was a huge success and ushered in a series of Christmas tales. It was read in households up and down the length of Britain and America, becoming something of an institution. It was said to have directly influenced the way people treated each other around this special time of year – an American factory-owner gave his employees an extra day's holiday, for example. The miserly character of Ebeneezer

An image of Ebeneezer Scrooge, from Dickens's fantastically successful *A Christmas Carol*, written in 1843. This short story was to be the first of several tales set at this time of year.

Dickens and Christmas

Charles Dickens is often credited as single-handedly inventing the modern Christmas, with its appeal to our childhood, its turkey and stuffing, holly and mistletoe, its family gatherings, the carols, Christmas tree, presents and all the good will. This is to some extent true and is illustrated in an **anecdote** from the poet and novelist Theodore Watts-Duncan. He tells how, on hearing of the death of Charles Dickens, a barrow girl in London's Covent Garden exclaimed, 'then will Father Christmas die too?' However, the **Victorian** Christmas had started before Dickens had become famous.

Scrooge was so vivid that the term 'Scrooge' has entered the language to describe people of a similar disposition. It was an unashamedly sentimental and manipulative story, using the characters and events to make a point, but it worked a treat! It took under two months to write and was the first story he had written that was never serialized.

An extended break

Dickens needed a break from work. He decided that he would take his family off to Italy, letting out their house in Devonshire Terrace for the duration of their stay abroad. They embarked from Dover in July 1844 as a family party of twelve (including two domestic servants). They took a large coach across Europe. From Boulogne to Paris, a city Dickens fell in love with ('I cannot conceive any place so perfectly and wonderfully expressive of its own character,' he said of the magical place), they went on through France, stopping at Lyon, Avignon and Marseille, from where they set sail for Italy. Genoa was a disappointment, but they took a villa there. Italy held the delights of Parma, Modena, Bologna, Ferrara, Venice, Rome and more. Dickens was to write 'Pictures from Italy' about his travels in the country. He returned to England in December, to work, but was then back in Italy until July 1845.

A diverse life

Back in England, Dickens helped start a newspaper, the *Daily News*, in which his 'Pictures from Italy' piece appeared. It was a short-lived venture from his point of view – he only remained as **editor** for a little under three weeks, though the paper itself continued running. In 1845, he also started up an amateur theatrical company. This was to take up a lot of his time over the coming years. He had written a second Christmas story for December 1844 (*The Chimes*), and a third followed in December 1845 (*The Cricket on the Hearth*). He was back abroad in 1846, this time travelling in Switzerland. Here he started work on his next novel, *Dombey and Son*, which was serialized throughout that year, with the last piece published in April 1848.

A very creative period

These middle years of Dickens's life were extremely creative. He was to write some of his greatest pieces of fiction from his late thirties onwards. These include the most **autobiographical** of his novels, *David Copperfield* (1849–50), *Bleak House* (1852–53), *Hard Times* (1854), *Little Dorrit* (1855–57), *A Tale of Two Cities* (1859) and *Great Expectations* (1860–61). He was still finding time to tour abroad – in 1853 he went back to Italy, with Wilkie Collins, a friend and fellow novelist.

David Copperfield, as well as being strongly based on events in Dickens's own life, is held as a novel that makes a further shift in his

An illustration from Dickens's *Great Expectations*, published in serial form between 1860 and 1861. It shows the young hero of the book, Pip, with Joe Gargery.

writing, started in *Martin Chuzzlewit* (see page 42). Dickens uses a carefully planned structure much more obviously than in his earlier novels. He presents us with his hero, David Copperfield, going through a series of experiences that shape his character and help him develop greater understanding of himself and the world. *Hard Times* also reveals Dickens's shift in his style and sympathies. The sentimentality of the characters in his earlier works is almost gone, and he is moving towards a far more serious tone.

Dickens and realism

In the preface to *Oliver Twist* Dickens talks to us directly about his desire to show London life as it really was and not in some idealized form:

'I had read of thieves by the scores... but I never met... with the miserable reality... To show them as they really are, for ever skulking uneasily through the dirtiest paths of life, with the great, black, ghastly gallows closing up their prospects, turn them where they may; it appeared to me that to do this, would be to attempt a something which was greatly needed, and which would be a service to society.'

Some of the most memorable and atmospheric scenes from the novel are those set in the slums, or 'rookeries', that Fagin and his child criminals, such as the Artful Dodger, inhabit.

This new approach is continued in the novel *Great Expectations*. Here, the book's hero, Pip, is seen going through three stages in his life – his childhood in Kent, time as a young man in London and a period of dark disillusionment at the end of the novel. Pip moves closer to self-awareness and finds that all his worldly desires only lead to discontent.

Dickens at work

One of the most notable things about a Dickens novel is the great range of characters it contains. Dickens created dozens for each novel. By this period, he had perfected his techniques. There are numerous references to Dickens speaking aloud in his study while writing the **dialogue** for his characters. He said that he could get inside each character, rather like an actor would, to feel how they would act and react to other people and situations. He could hear their voices in his head, their way of speaking, their accents, their **mannerisms**, the class background that their language betrayed. All these things combined in Dickens to make him the greatest creator of memorable people in the English novel.

Another aspect of a Dickens novel is the tremendous atmosphere he creates. The reader cannot help but be affected by the descriptions of

Miss Haversham and her house in *Great Expectations*, or the Courts of Chancery in *Bleak House*. The 19th-century critic G K Chesterton said that a 'characteristic of Dickens [is] that his atmospheres are more important than his stories'. Part of getting the atmosphere right was in his acute attention to detail. Dickens was fanatical about describing streets and lanes in London accurately, as he was with all his scenes. For example, when writing a scene set on the north Kent marshes for *Great Expectations*, he hired a small steamboat for the day, from which to explore the area. He wanted the realism to come through from first-hand knowledge.

A photograph of the older Dickens with his daughters, Katie and Mary (Mamie). It was taken in the garden of the house he bought in 1856, Gad's Hill Place, in Kent.

Gad's Hill Place

Dickens was fond of rebuilding his childhood. He bought back all the books that as a child he had been made to sell off when the family were in debt, for example. A symbolic gesture in this direction was his purchase in 1856 of the large house Gad's Hill Place, near Rochester in Kent. He had passed it with his father many times as a child, and so was very familiar with its exterior. He said in later life that his father had promised that one day he would have enough money to buy such a house, if only he worked hard enough. Now, all these years later, through sheer will power, Charles was able to make good on that idle promise. He paid £1790 for the house, and the family spent

Dickens in his library, painted by Clarkson Stanfield. The library was an important space for Dickens. It represented his beloved world of books as well as quiet, solitude or conversation with another literary friend.

Dickens the dandy

From an early age Charles developed a careful approach to his clothes. He was always keen to be seen smartly turned out. In later, wealthier, life this tipped over into dandyism. He was often to be seen at important functions dressed with a lot of jewellery, colourful waistcoats and his hair long for the period. Some people thought this was vulgar. Thackeray once wrote, on seeing him at a ball, 'how splendid Mrs Dickens was in pink satin and Mr Dickens in geranium and ringlets'.

their first summer there in 1857. It was during that summer that they were visited by the Danish poet and writer of fairytales, Hans Christian Andersen.

Separation

1858 was an eventful year for the Dickenses. Charles launched upon what was to prove a well-paid series of public readings. He had read aloud before, but not for money. He started in London, but was eventually to visit all parts of Britain and even America. He also quarrelled in this year with his friend and fellow novelist, William Makepeace Thackeray. However, all these matters were slight in comparison with a major event at this time – his separation from Catherine.

He had been growing apart from Catherine for many years. They were temperamentally very different people – he was exuberant, moody, something of a dandy (see box above), tyrannical on occasions, and of course a gifted writer of the highest order. She was given to prolonged periods of depression, out of which he seemed unable to lift her. Another factor in this was his meeting Ellen Ternan, an actress, in 1857. She was a member of the cast in one of his productions. They would have had plenty of opportunity to get to know each other well during rehearsals and performances.

The death of Charles Dickens

The 1860s brought the now ageing Dickens more than his fair share of stress and hard work. He had launched a new weekly magazine in 1859, called *All the Year Round*, which proved a big success. He published his instalments of *A Tale of Two Cities* in it. The years 1861 and 1862 saw him giving a gruelling series of public readings in London. The following year he was in Paris doing the same.

A gruesome ordeal

Dickens was unwell a lot of the time now. He had a kidney condition that was probably giving him high blood pressure. He went to Paris with Ellen Ternan in May 1865 for a rest. He was working on finishing the last instalments of *Our Mutual Friend*. While returning through the Kent countryside by train, he and the actress were caught up in a terrible accident. Works were being carried out on a viaduct (a bridge-like structure), but the foreman had looked at the wrong timetable. When the train carrying Dickens appeared, the line was up. It was unable to stop in time and became derailed. There were many casualties, though Dickens's carriage remained intact. However, he did help with the wounded and the dying, and was haunted by the event for the rest of his life.

An engraving of Dickens helping the wounded in a railway accident near Staplehurst in Kent, on 9 June 1865. The accident disturbed him greatly, although he was physically unhurt.

Declining health

In spite of pain and a lack of his usual energy, Dickens still drove himself as he always had done. He undertook a reading tour in America during 1867–68 and returned exhausted. In 1869 he collapsed with a mild stroke after a reading tour that had taken him to Scotland and Ireland. He immediately cancelled all further engagements for the time being. However, he embarked upon what was to be his last novel, *The Mystery of Edwin Drood*. It was after a full day working on this that he suffered a more serious stroke, at home at Gad's Hill Place, on 8 June 1870. He died the next day.

Westminster Abbey

'The great king of fiction is dead! The mighty intellect that bred ten thousand pleasant fancies, the wondrous power that moved men's hearts to Joy or grief, and led the world captive… is at rest.' So ran part of a tribute to Charles Dickens in *The Hornet* newspaper on 15 June 1870. It was one of many tributes paid shortly after Dickens's death. He had delighted people from all levels of society with his humour and outrageous characters. He was given the highest honour a nation could give to a writer, and buried in Poets' Corner in Westminster Abbey. Dickens had taken his place alongside the nation's greatest poets and dramatists.

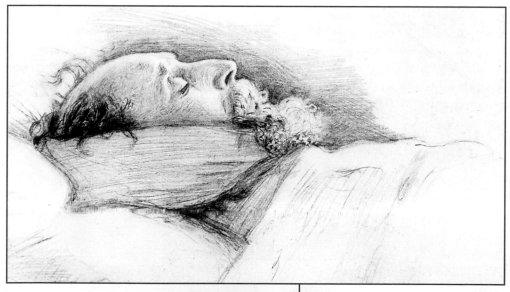

This touching portrait of Dickens was sketched by J.M. Millais after the novelist's death at Gad's Hill Place in 1870.

The legacy of Charles Dickens

Dickens had bridged a difficult gap between literature and the mass of ordinary readers. The sales of his works were enormous for the period – the last issue of *The Pickwick Papers* sold 40,000 copies. He had become an instant success and held on to his audience throughout his career. He showed future writers of the novel just how serious subject matter could be combined with the comic and popular, giving something for almost everybody to read, think about and enjoy. Shakespeare had achieved the same degree of all-encompassing writing in his plays 250 years earlier, deliberately aiming to entertain a wide range of society. As one critic said about Dickens: 'there is no contemporary writer whose works are read so generally through the whole house, who can give pleasure to the servants as well as the mistress, to the children as well as to the master'.

Dickens also achieved a high degree of realism in his novels, especially the later ones, pointing the direction in which the novel was to go. He kept his love of the theatrical, the stage effect, the exaggerated and the absurd throughout his works, but the depth and **psychological** perception in them intensified. In many ways, novelists writing in the English language live in the shadow of this man, just as all dramatists live in the shadow of Shakespeare.

Dickens and morality

Dickens reached and influenced a wider audience around the world than any other

A painting by Robert William Bass. It shows the author day-dreaming in his study with many of the characters from his novels coming out of his imagination and inhabiting the room.

An engraving of Dickens reading aloud from the second of his Christmas stories, *The Chimes*, published December 1844. His skills as a reader are clear from the expressions on the faces of his audience.

living author at the time. He was conscious of his power and importance as a writer and took the role of educator seriously. He worked hard to give meaning to his work (occasionally assuming a rather **didactic** tone, which detracts from the writing), and to show his readers that moral and political concerns were ultimately rooted in the individual and the day-to-day decisions they took. His readers were affected, and no doubt Dickens did alter their responses to things going on around them and to the way they treated each other.

For Dickens wrote supremely well about financial greed. He saw this within institutions such as the law, local authorities, and even the Church itself. He also wrote about the only force that could counteract its evil influence – love. Love in a family, between friends, love simply for the rest of humanity. His novels are full of the ordinary humour and strength of character that sees people through the most appalling situations. This was appreciated by the audiences of his day. He holds up the virtues of self-sacrifice, loyalty and trust, and sets them against the excesses of industrial greed and the pursuit of profit.

In our own time, these fundamental issues have not changed, which is one of the reasons Charles Dickens remains such a well-loved and important writer. The power of his language, characterization, scene-setting and use of atmosphere have all made his work so timeless, whilst it remains deeply rooted in the **Victorian** period.

Dickens in other media

Dickens's work has translated very successfully into other media. Many of his books have been made into films, plays, serials on television, or musicals. These include *Oliver Twist*, *Great Expectations*, *David Copperfield*, *Nicholas Nickleby*, *A Christmas Carol* and *Our Mutual Friend*. Indeed, *Dombey and Son* was given its first stage performance only three years after Dickens's death. The sense of history and place in his stories is very strong, and this has attracted directors, as have the powerful story lines. Their wide public appeal carries over into other media – it stems from the story line being so broad, encompassing so many diverse people, from all walks of life. The fact that most of his books were written for serialization may also play a part in their attraction. His use of the 'cliff-hanger' as a device to get readers eagerly anticipating the next instalment is something that can be made use of by those directing his works on television or film.

Abel Magwitch, the escaped convict, meets with the young Pip on the north Kent marshes – a scene from Twentieth Century Fox's film adaptation of Dickens's *Great Expectations*.

Dickens's own life

Dickens had a very disadvantaged start in life and won through to fame, wealth and general public acclaim through sheer hard work, will power and a stroke of genius. He never lost his compassion for the poor and weak in society or his utter contempt for the hypocritical, the pompous, the cruel and the arrogant. He may have been a sad and worn out old man at the end of his life, but he remained true to the ideals of the young man in him, setting out on an adventure in life and in words. He won through to a unique position in English literature – his works have remained classics, studied at universities all over the world; but they have also retained their popular appeal, bought by everyone to be entertained, moved to tears and laughter, and to be shown the highs and lows of life.

A complex legacy

Being the complex and energetic man that he was, Charles Dickens's legacy has a great many sides to it. He not only wrote about the burning issues of Victorian society but was directly involved with many of them. He campaigned for charities, including educational institutions and orphanages, never forgetting the hardship of his own upbringing. He fought for the rights of authors through international **copyright**. He was an ardent supporter of amateur theatricals. He reported with a depth of humanity on many political subjects of the day, but never became attached to a political party, preferring to keep his distance and individuality intact throughout. He was in correspondence with some of the most powerful individuals of the day – **aristocrats**, politicians and literary figures. He has left us around 14,000 handwritten letters, sent to people from all walks of society and about topics of public and private interest. He could not help but leave behind a fundamental influence upon those who knew him directly, and those who had not met him but had had their hearts and lives touched by his fiction.

This influence continues today. Because Dickens captured what it meant to live in Victorian Britain so vividly, he has become the greatest symbol of his age.

1845 *The Cricket on the Hearth* published.
Birth of son Alfred.

1846 Writes 'Pictures from Italy'.

1846-47 Further travels in Europe, including Italy, Switzerland and France.
Sets up and briefly edits the *Daily News*.
Birth of son Sydney.

1848 *Dombey and Son* published.
Death of Dickens's sister Fanny.

1849 Birth of son Henry.

1850 *David Copperfield* published.
Begins publishing *Household Words* (weekly magazine).
Birth of daughter Dora.
William Wordsworth, **Poet Laureate**, and one of the main Romantic poets, dies. Alfred Tennyson is appointed new Poet Laureate.

1851 Death of Dickens's father, John.
Death of daughter, Dora.

1852 Birth of son Edward.

1853 *Bleak House* published.
Starts public reading career.

1854 *Hard Times* published.

1855 Lives in Paris for a few months.
Directs and acts in play by his friend Wilkie Collins –
The Lighthouse.

1856 Buys Gad's Hill Place in Kent.

1857 *Little Dorrit* published.
Directs and acts in *The Frozen Deep*, another play by Wilkie Collins.
Meets actress Ellen Ternan.

1858 Leaves his wife, Catherine.

1859 *A Tale of Two Cities* published.
Begins publishing *All the Year Round* (weekly magazine).
Samuel Smiles publishes *Self-help*, a book that sums up the values of the **Victorian middle classes**, preaching hardwork, thrift and self-improvement as the best ways out of the poverty trap.

1860   Dickens's **autobiographical** essays, called 'The Uncommercial Traveller', published in *All the Year Round*.

1861   *Great Expectations* published.

1863   William Makepeace Thackery, novelist and one-time friend of Dickens, dies. They had quarrelled in later life, but had made up their differences.

1865   *Our Mutual Friend* published.
Dickens is involved in a rail accident near Staplehurst in Kent, but is physically unhurt.

1867-68 Dickens does farewell reading tour of North America. Has a slight stroke which cuts short his tour.

1868   Benjamin Disraeli becomes prime minister.
Disraeli was also a novelist having published *Vivian Grey* in 1826.

1869   Dickens suffers another mild stroke whilst on a reading tour in the UK.

1870   Has a private audience with one of his great admirers, Queen Victoria, at Buckingham Palace.
Starts writing *The Mystery of Edwin Drood*.
Gives his last public reading, of *A Christmas Carol*, in March.
Dies 9 June.
He is buried at Westminster Abbey.

Glossary

anecdote short account of an event that has happened to somebody

aristocracy highest rank in society, next to the king and queen and their family

autobiography factual book that someone writes about their life

bankrupt having no money or means left to pay debts

Baptist minister leader of the Baptist church, a form of Protestantism that originated amongst some British people living in Holland in the early 17th century

capitalism name given to a system of economics based on competition and profit

catalyst someone or something that triggers off an event or change

chandler someone who runs a business supplying all the needs for a ship about to go on a voyage

copyright legal ownership of a work of fiction (or other artistic work). This is usually belongs to the person who writes the work.

creditor someone that is owed money by someone else. If a person goes bankrupt, they are unable to pay their creditors.

dialogue speech between two or more people

didactic when something teaches or instructs, rather than simply entertains

editor person who runs and puts together a newspaper or someone who works on text for a publishing company

evict to throw someone out of their home due to non-payment of rent

farce comedy that uses the ridiculous and far-fetched to make people laugh

Great Reform Act Act passed by Parliament in 1832 that gave the vote to more people (about 220,000 extra voters). The new voters came from the middle classes, who through the Industrial Revolution had become wealthier and more powerful than ever before.

guinea gold coin used in Britain at the time of Dickens, valued at around 21 shillings (just over £1)

Industrial Revolution name given to the period in British history between about 1750 and 1850 in which machinery increasingly came to replace human labour, typified by the use of steam power in factories

infant mortality number of deaths per year amongst infants per thousand that are born

Inns of Court places near the Law Courts in London where law students used to live. They include Lincoln's Inn, Gray's Inn, Inner Temple and Middle Temple.

Liberal in Dickens's day, a member of the Liberal Party, which favoured reform and progress. The party was known as the Whig Party before the 1840s.

mannerism something that is special or odd about a person in terms of the way they dress, speak or conduct themselves

marine insurance type of business dealing with shipping. Vessels were insured for their value and that of their cargo. In the event of an accident, most of the loss was paid for by the insurance companies.

melodrama popular form of play that included lots of exaggerated emotion, unrealistic plots, obvious villains, and happy endings

middle class section of society between the working class and the aristocracy. In Dickens's time this class expanded considerably and became divided into lower and upper middle classes.

mimicry ability to imitate something or someone

music hall popular place for entertainment, including songs, dance, melodrama and comedy. Music halls started in towns and cities in Britain in the 1830s and 1840s.

parish district that has its own church

pathos something in a work of art that moves a person to feel the emotion of pity

periodical newspaper or magazine that appears usually once a week or month (sometimes less often), rather than on a daily basis

pirate edition printing of a book for which the author or copyright owner has not given permission

Poet Laureate poet appointed to the royal household who writes poems on special royal and national occasions

proof copies of a book produced before it is printed, for the author to make final changes

pseudonym alternative name somebody uses when they publish something. For example, Dickens used the name Boz instead of his own name on the cover of some of his early books.

psychological to do with mental processes and behaviour

ragged school type of school developed from 1818 by John Pounds, a shoemaker, to give some education to poor and underprivileged children in Britain. The schools did not charge any fee.

reform to change or redo something. In Dickens's time, many laws were being reformed to make way for new ideas coming mainly from the middle classes.

sanitation systems that bring fresh water supplies and remove human waste

shorthand system of writing, using squiggle-like symbols, that allows a person to keep up with writing what someone is saying

sketch quick drawing or written outline of something

smallpox disease that was widespread in Europe during Dickens's lifetime. A smallpox vaccine was discovered in the early 19th century, which eventually led to its control.

soap opera sentimental and popular form of television or radio programme, usually in serial form, centred on the lives of so-called 'ordinary' people

urban relating to towns and cities

urinary organs organs such as the kidneys that deal with urine (a waste product) and help the body to get rid of it

Victorian in British history, term describing the period that covers the reign of Queen Victoria, which lasted from 1837 till her death in 1901

Whig member of the Whig Party that emerged in the 18th century, mainly from the merchant classes. It became the Liberal Party in the years after the Great Reform Act was passed.

working class people in a society whose only source of income is their labour, who have no money to invest in stocks or shares

writers' guilds groups set up for the support of fledgling writers

Places of interest
and further reading

Places to visit

Bleak House, Broadstairs, Kent, UK – a Dickens museum containing Victorian items and Dickens memorabilia.

Charles Dickens Birthplace Museum, Portsmouth, Hampshire, UK – contains much of interest surrounding Dickens's life and times.

The Dickens Fellowship – founded 1902. Its headquarters are at The Dickens House Museum (see below) or visit *www.dickens.fellowship.btinternet.co.uk*

The Dickens House Museum, 48 Doughty Street, London WC1N 2LX Tel: 020 7405 2127, *www.dickensmuseum.com* – a museum dedicated to the life of Dickens. Contains rooms kept as they were during his life.

National Portrait Gallery, St Martin's Place, London WC2H 0HE – contains portraits of Charles Dickens and other prominent Victorians.

Websites

www.bbc.co.uk/education/webguide – Search under 'Dickens' for links to loads of information, including discussions of his works and famous quotes.

www.dickensfoundation.org – has links to other sites, including information on the Dickens family tree.

Further reading

Any of Charles Dickens's novels. The Penguin editions generally have good, informative introductions. You could also try:

Living Through History: Britain 1750–1900, Nigel Kelly, Rosemary Rees, Jane Shuter (Heinemann Library, 1998)

The Age of Industry, Andrew Langley (Hamlyn, 1994)

Chartism, Bob Rees (Heinemann Library, 1995)

Life in a Victorian House, Laura Wilson (Hamlyn, 1993)

Sources

Dickens, Peter Ackroyd (Guild Publishing, 1990)

The Penguin Dickens Companion, Paul Davis (Penguin Books, 1999)

Dickens: A Biography, Fred Kaplan (Hodder & Stoughton, 1988)

Charles Dickens, Catherine Peters (Sutton Publishing Ltd, 1998)

Index

Titles in the *Creative Lives* series:

Hardback   0 431 13985 7

Hardback   0 431 13982 2

Hardback   0 431 13983 0

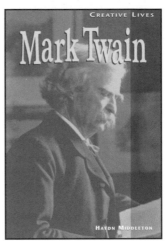

Hardback   0 431 13980 6

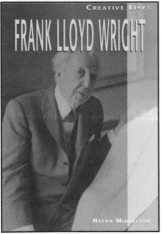

Hardback   0 431 13981 4

Find out about other Heinemann resources on our website www.heinemann.co.uk/library